THE SPIRITUAL PATH OF PURPOSE

A Journal for Purposeful Living

JOHN HORAN-KATES

To order additional copies of this book, contact:
Xlibris
844-714-8691
www.Xlibris.com
Orders@Xlibris.com

Scripture quotations marked KJV are from the Holy Bible, King
James Version (Authorized Version). First published in 1611.
Quoted from the KJV Classic Reference Bible, Copyright © 1983
by The Zondervan Corporation.

ISBN: Softcover   978-1-6698-2061-1
       Hardcover   978-1-6698-2062-8
       EBook   978-1-6698-2060-4

Print information available on the last page

Rev. date: 04/12/2022

Contents

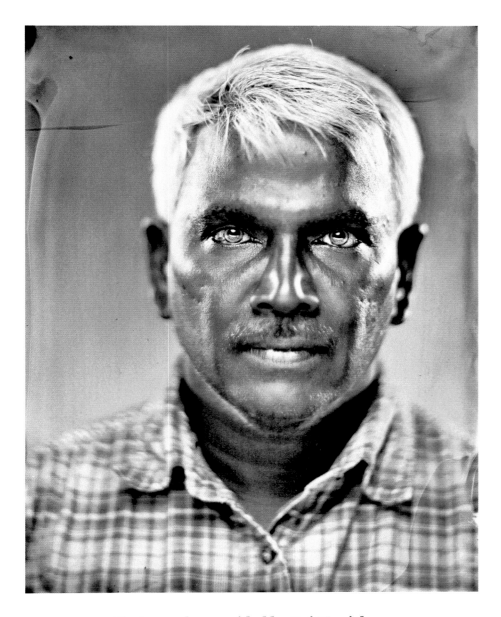

Photography provided by Raj Manickam

AllinGoodLight.com

Dedication

I dedicate this book to my mother, Bessie Virdin Kates, who started me on my spiritual journey in 1957 at a Billy Graham rally at Detroit's cavernous Masonic Auditorium. When his alter call came, I said to myself, "I'm not going up there – he's gonna make me cry." And so, I didn't, but that call nevertheless launched my spiritual joirney.

Thanks, Mom !

Bessie Virdin Kates in front of our Detroit home.

Foreword

The Spirit of Purpose

by Richard Leider

Your purpose.
Your reason for being.
Your reason for getting up in the morning.

You may not have contemplated the first two much, but most of us have occasionally wondered these days about our reason for getting up in the morning.

Why do *you* get up most mornings?

Purpose motivates us to get up in the morning to do what we do. Purpose is an expression of our deepest values. It is the spirit around which we orient our time and daily choices. It's the reason we were born.

John Horan-Kates has lived in the purpose question for decades. And, through study and practice he has become a seasoned and trusted leader to guide us on our purpose journey. What determines the power of purpose is the worthiness of its aim. Purpose requires an aim beyond ourselves. John's aim is clear and compelling: to help us live purposefully.

Purpose is not a luxury. It is fundamental to life. Like health and money, it is essential to our longevity and happiness. Naming and claiming our purpose helps us satisfy our hunger to matter-to know that we are living a life that we deem to be worth our time on earth. Mattering matters.

There is no one and never will be anyone just like you. Each of us is an experiment of ONE! We were each born with the spirit of purpose-an innate desire to leave our footprints, our unique contribution to life. We can learn from, but not adopt, the purpose of another person. We must uncover, discover, and rediscover our own way.

This journal inspires and guides us to do just that. Purpose is age-agnostic. It is not discovered just once and then we are done with it. It is reexamined at various ages, often during crises and life transitions.

This personal and practical journal gets to the heart of how purpose shapes us and how we can shape it. It gently nudges us to get on and to stay on the spiritual path of purpose.

Richard Leider is a bestselling author of *The Power of Purpose, Repacking Your Bags, and Life Reimagined*. His most recent book is *Who Do you Want to be When You Grow Old: The Path of Purposeful Aging. His company is* **The Inventure Group**

Introduction

The Spiritual Path of Purpose is a journal intended to inspire your thoughts about the important process of finding and experiencing a purposeful life. The fifty-three chapters suggests a week-by-week exercise to expose significant quotations, what they imply to me, and to encourage your response through a series of questions.

The inspiration for this book came from the Bible in Matthew 23:26 where Jesus says, "First cleanse the inside...that the outside may be clean as well." When I was reminded of this phrase in the middle of one night, the concept of a purposeful living curriculum was born. Starting on the inside first spoke volumes to me. It said, examine the softer aspects of one's character before promoting the outside skills. "Inside First™" became a series of small group development initiatives that emphasized assessing one's values, gifts, talents and passions first.

This approach then led to the examination of one's purpose on the assumption that clarity on these important dimensions of one's character could guide one's life. Once the inside qualities were clear, then the classic skills of planning, communication, team-building and all the other central faculties could be examined, having first clarified one's character.

In the course of this process, the important aspect of one's spiritual perspective would invariably come up. Without advocating any particular flavor or doctrine, people would express whatever influence their upbringing had on their spiritual worldview. This kind of open conversation in small groups of 6 to 7 would often lead to a clearer sense of each person's purpose or direction in life.

After about twenty years of leading these small groups, I concluded that a weekly journal addressing the importance of this "spiritual path" might be helpful to fellow travelers. I hope you find it beneficial.

John Horan-Kates
Vail Valley, Colorado

P.S. Here's an introduction I used in one of my earlier books that relates to purposeful living !

I Choose to Be Purposeful...

I will not wander aimlessly,
For my life is too valuable to squander.
I promise to develop my talents,
to nurture my dreams,
and to strive to understand
what God intends for my life.
I sense clarity here will not come easily,
but you can count on me
to shape a meaningful and inspiring purpose for my life !

Session 1: Inquiry

"The unexamined life is not worth living."

Socrates

Socrates is calling us to examine our lives – something too many of us do rarely, if at all. What's required in a good inquiry and why be bothered?

Much like the typical annual physical exam, a life exam should be done at least annually – maybe even quarterly. For those among us who have a "life plan" it usually includes financial goals, professional activities, retirement activity, wills and trusts, and other important elements of one's life. While these are important considerations, I think Socrates is pointing at something deeper – like purpose and vision.

Examining one's life purpose goes to the root of who we are as a person. What do you stand for, what do you really pay attention to, what consumes you? These kinds of questions draw upon your talents and that to which you deeply hunger. If approached thoughtfully and reviewed regularly, your answers will inform those other goals and objectives you've identified. Your life plan will be based on what's really important.

The same applies to the writing of a vision statement. Typically, casting a vision can be described as what it will look like when you are achieving your life's purpose. Who will be with you, where will you be, and what does it feel like? Visioning is your opportunity to make specific your dreams and aspirations.

Examining your purpose and your vision regularly will keep your focused on what's most important.

Socrates was a Greek philosopher from Athens who is credited as a founder of Western philosophy and the first moral philosopher of the Western ethical tradition of thought.

Today's Journal

When you last really examined your life, what did you discover?

_____
_____
_____
_____
_____
_____
_____
_____

Can you describe a vision for your next chapter?

_____
_____
_____
_____
_____
_____
_____
_____

Action Step – What will you do with these thoughts? And, by when?

_____
_____
_____

Session 2: Commitment

"Purpose is a profound commitment to a compelling
expectation for the time of your life."

Frederic Hudson

Yes, it's definitely profound. It's very rare that a young person will come-up with a purpose that stays with them throughout life – but it can happen. It's more likely that as the chapters of our lives unfold, changes in residence, employment, marital status, etc. our perspectives on purpose evolve. Some would describe that as maturity.

When I was single, living in San Francisco, my purpose – although I didn't call it that – was to find the right woman. It was more of a goal – even an immediate objective. But, as I passed through my twenties, I started to realize I needed to think a bit more long-term. Getting married, realizing I wasn't on my own anymore, that there's someone else to consider, really caused me to think about my future and what I really wanted.

That life-changing event was when the notion of commitment became real for me. As Frederic Hudson notes above, I had made "a compelling commitment" to another person. I began to think about and talk with my wife about what kind of life we wanted – "we" being the operative word. Through reading and participating in a variety of personal development workshops and seminars, my eyes were opened to various possibilities.

As time went on, children arrived that provided a whole new set of commitments that influenced my evolving perspective. What did I want for them and how would that change my outlook. But each step along the way, I began to see a pattern. I saw that my thinking was coalescing around something more enduring – something that gave me a direction.

A purpose statement for my life didn't take real shape until I was in my forties. And even since then, it's morphed and tightened and become more specific. It's evolved as I've matured. I often wonder where I'd be if I had started on this purpose journey much earlier. But in the end, I'm of the opinion that that Supreme Being had a hand in each of the twists and turns along the way.

Frederic Hudson is the author of *LifeLaunch* and *The Adult Years.* He was the founder of the **Hudson Institute of Coaching** in Santa Barbara.

Today's Journal

How has your outlook on life evolved?

_____

_____

_____

_____

_____

_____

_____

_____

_____

What are you really committed to?

_____

_____

_____

_____

_____

_____

_____

_____

Action Step – What will you do with these thoughts? And, by when?

_____

_____

_____

Session 3: Understanding

*"There are two kinds of people. Those who seek certainty
and those who seek understanding."*

Richard Rohr

I am the kind of person who is much more about seeking understanding than certainty. To me, certainty – knowing exactly what is right or wrong, what is fact versus story – can be problematic. Religious fundamentalists draw upon their doctrine which they know to be right. I'm a life-long learner who is just trying to ask good questions – who is seeking understanding – who is trying to find meaning in words and concepts.

Somewhere along the way – and I think it might have come from Richard Rohr – I came to see my life as a continuum with responsibility on one end and surrender on the other. Responsibility is a key word for me since it indicates that I intend to carry out what I've promised to do. That notion was just woven into my way of doing things – perhaps from my experience in the Navy in Vietnam.

The other end of that spectrum is the notion of surrender. Surrender is one of those words most of us don't like. It sounds like losing; and who cherishes that? But I have found another way to understand that concept. It's not about giving up, but rather about realizing that I'm not in control of the outcome in any transaction or situation. The Big Guy upstairs is in control. When I recognized this, everything became more clear – and I stopped worrying about the outcome so much. But I didn't give up either because that would be counter to taking responsibility.

As you reflect on whether your purpose is right for you, just know that as you move along your life path, various doors will be open for you and others will be closed. Go through the open door because that's the door that God is directing you to. Trying to go through a closed door will just hurt. In fact, I pray that He would light that door so I won't miss it, even to the use of a Hollywood klieg light.

Richard Rohr is the author of *Falling Upward, Breathing Under Water, A Spirit Within Us* and many others. He is the founder of the **Center for Action & Contemplation** in Albuquerque, New Mexico.

Today's Journal

How do you understand the idea of "surrender?"

_____

_____

_____

_____

_____

_____

_____

_____

_____

How does the notion of responsibility fit into your worldview?

_____

_____

_____

_____

_____

_____

_____

_____

Action Step – What will you do with these thoughts? And, by when?

_____

_____

_____

Session 4: Inside First

"First cleanse the inside...that the outside may be clean as well."

Jesus of Nazareth

Going inside first is an excellent path to begin the journey of finding your purpose. It's on the inside – in the heart – where the important dimensions of our self-concept reside. It's where our values – what we hold most dear – dwell. It's in the heart where our passions well-up. That's the place where our emotions originate. The things that drive us deep are feelings, beliefs and attitudes.

The process is about asking yourself a lot of questions. Some Saturday, find a quiet place, maybe outside under a tree, and with a notebook or tablet, start to record your thoughts. This will be a soul-searching exercise where you go inside – into your deepest place – your heart.

One of the most central questions is, "What makes you come alive?" By that I mean, when are you really paying attention to something? What grabs your interest with a tight grip. Then ask this question; "What do you lose yourself in?" For me, it's being outside in God's creation. Whether walking, riding a bike or skiing a powder run, that activity typically has my full attention. What is that for you?

Other questions to consider are, "What are your strengths?" "What are your gifts, talents and abilities?" "When are you most energetic and fulfilled?" It's helpful to write down your answers to each of these questions. As you note the words that describe your answers, look for connections of these words with the concept of purpose. What do they tell you about the direction you might take?

Another query might be to think about what people regularly come to you for. What is it that they see in you that attracts them? Is it some expertise or your experience? Again, make a few notes about this. Lastly, in the publications you read, what issues interest you? What draws your eye and what do you skip over automatically?

As these are important inside-first questions, it will be valuable to give them adequate attention over the coming months !

Jesus of Nazareth didn't write any books that we know of, but the entire *New Testament* is about him.

Today's Journal

What are some key words you've been using in your reflections in this journal?

_____

_____

_____

_____

_____

_____

_____

_____

_____

What does "inside first" mean to you?

_____

_____

_____

_____

_____

_____

_____

_____

Action Step – What will you do with these thoughts? And, by when?

_____

_____

_____

Session 5: Purposeful

"Purposeful people are doing the work they love, with people they care about, in a place where they belong."

Richard Leider

Can this really be achieved? Who are these people?

I can speak from experience – yes you can achieve this end. But, I didn't get there right away. It took me many years of thinking and planning – and praying.

At first, I thought that marketing was the work that I loved. I enjoyed the creative aspect of the job, particularly the conceiving of big events. But much later in that initial career I realized it was the people that I met and worked with that I loved. Fun people, enjoying life, engaged in interesting things. Some were well known, but most were regular people who could be friends – people I cared about.

The place where I belonged was easier. Right out of the Navy, I found myself in the mountains. First in the California High Sierra, but within two years, I had landed in Colorado. Within a few years, I was VP of Marketing for Vail and I was in heaven. Then marriage and two children helped to cement "the place" question for me.

During my life-seminars phase, I came to realize that my purpose was to "build community." In various ways, I was definitely doing that – building organizations, facilities and relationships.

Then, my facilitation of a number of small groups helped me go deeper. I wasn't pushing any agenda; I was just asking people to take time to examine their life – to go deep. Every time I did this, I realized I had just introduced the spiritual into the process without preaching. Since that day's work had been around writing their purpose statements, I was helping connect them to their deeper selves.

Richard Leider is author of *The Power of Purpose, Life Reimagined, Repacking Your Bags* and *Who Do You Want to Be When You Grow Old – The Path of Purposeful Aging.*

Today's Journal

Where do you stand on those three parts of Leider's statement above? Work, people and place.

_____

_____

_____

_____

_____

_____

_____

_____

_____

How do you feel about inviting a spiritual perspective into your purpose?

_____

_____

_____

_____

_____

_____

_____

_____

Action Step – What will you do with these thoughts? And, by when?

_____

_____

_____

Session 6: Worldview

*"The condition of our hearts, the openness of our attitudes, the
quality of our competence, the fidelity of our experience – these
give vitality to the work experience and meaning to life."*

Max DePree

I think DePree is describing here what I'd call your worldview. It's how you see things from the broadest, all encompassing, perspective.

The condition of your heart is probably most important. Is it open and positive looking out at the world for what's good? Or is it caught-up with doubts and concerns? Is it healthy and capable of withstanding challenges? Or is it weak and under attack?

The openness of your attitudes speaks to your disposition and personality. Are you an either/or guy, or a both/and person? Richard Rohr calls this latter perspective "non-dual." Is being right something precious to you, or are you open to other viewpoints? Are you a lifelong learner, or is knowledge and information not that important?

Lastly, the fidelity of your experience, what you've been through, what you've endured, speaks to the breadth of your worldview. If you have twenty years or more experience, that provides – hopefully – some wisdom. Has your experience been positive and worth remembering? Have you recovered from a challenging experience, or does it continue to haunt you?

All of these factors – and various others – contribute to meaning in your life. What more do you need to make it a meaningful and purposeful life?

Max DePree is the author of *Leadership is an Art* and *Leading Without Power*.

Today's Journal

How would you describe the condition of your heart?

_____

_____

_____

_____

_____

_____

_____

_____

What are the most important elements of your worldview?

_____

_____

_____

_____

_____

_____

_____

_____

Action Step – What will you do with these thoughts? And, by when?

_____

_____

_____

Session 7: Pilgrimage

"The world needs people with the patience and the passion to make a pilgrimage not only for their own sake but also as a social and political act. The world still waits for the truth that will set us free – my truth, your truth, our truth – the truth that was seeded in the earth when each of us arrived here formed in the image of God. Cultivating that truth, I believe, is the authentic vocation of every human being."

Parker Palmer

How do I gain spiritual maturity?

The author answers this question in the very first line – it takes patience. For many of us, it takes a lifetime because it's a process, or as Palmer says, it's a pilgrimage.

Regardless of our upbringings, most of us were introduced to religion at an early age. For some, it took hold. For others, it was elusive. Almost always, it was mostly about rules, practices and consequences. For me, the spiritual dimension of life didn't come into play until much later.

Seeking the truth at first seemed to me to be what education was all about. But in the early years it was knowledge that was being pushed. Remembering facts and information and being able to regurgitate it was rewarded. It wasn't until I completed my military service, got married and built a home that I had the time and inclination to advance the pilgrimage.

That pilgrimage included a series of personal development seminars and workshops over the next twenty years. Each event offered the opportunity to reflect on what I was up to and where I was headed. I was able to look inside – to look deeply at what I believed and valued. Stepping back from the day-to-day pressures was life-changing. It gave me the chance to cultivate that truth that Palmer refers to. And because I was able to reflect deeply, I developed a purpose for my life that still resonates today; "building spiritually-oriented community."

It took many years of nurturing my truths to gain spiritual maturity. And it has been worth all the effort.

Parker Palmer is the author of *Let Your Life Speak, A Hidden Wholeness* and *The Courage to Teach*. He is the founder of the **Center for Courage & Renewal**

Today's Journal

How would you describe the state of your spiritual maturity?

_____
_____
_____
_____
_____
_____
_____
_____

How patient are you?

_____
_____
_____
_____
_____
_____
_____
_____

Action Step – What will you do with these thoughts? And, by when?

_____
_____
_____

Session 8: Dynamism

"Spirituality is a dynamic process by which one discovers inner wisdom and vitality that gives meaning and purpose to all life events and relationships."

The Mayo Clinic

What might this dynamic process involve?

The first thing that I'm reminded of about this process is the time involved. And I'm not speaking of hours – but rather of years. Over those years as you mature, there'll be lots of hours spent in quiet reflection, but also lots of external experiences that shape your outlook on life.

For me, those times of reflection were spent answering questions posed by several wise elders. Some questions were specific, like, "What do you really care about?" Other questions were deeper, as in, "What gets you up in the morning?" Or, "What makes you come alive?"

That last question was posed in a statement by Howard Thurman, a noted spiritual visionary, who said, *"Don't ask yourself what the world needs. Ask yourself what makes you come alive, and go do that, because what the world needs is people who have come alive."*

That's such an important concept – helping people come alive – that I've devoted much of my last two decades to leading retreats that guide people in a process that allows each person to uncover those things for themselves. The key to the whole exercise is reflecting upon, and answering, meaningful questions. And it's dynamic, because sometimes those answers have evolved.

The Mayo Clinic is one of the world's leading medical organizations.

Today's Journal

What is that thing that makes you come alive?

_____

_____

_____

_____

_____

_____

_____

_____

What would allow you to do more of this?

_____

_____

_____

_____

_____

_____

_____

_____

Action Step – What will you do with these thoughts? And, by when?

_____

_____

_____

Session 9: Spiritual Beings

"Rather than thinking of ourselves as humans having a spiritual experience, think of yourself as a spiritual being having a human experience."

Wayne Dyer

Believing the Christian doctrine of eternal life helps, but it goes deeper than that. Being a spiritual being calls us to act with compassion in every situation we encounter. It's not an "on and off" switch, but rather a way of acting that comes from something deep within. Of course, no one's perfect, but as Vince Lombardi, former coach of the Green Bay Packers once said, "If we chase perfection and we might catch excellence."

But that calling – probably something connected to your purpose – doesn't come automatically as in some pre-packaged way. You've got to work at it. One of the "spiritual ways" of doing that is finding quiet time. Maybe you meditate or pray – the approach doesn't matter. When you're in that meditative state, see, feel and sense what comes up. Write it down. Don't reject stuff out-of-hand. Then later, review what you wrote. Or if it's just a word or two, consider developing that into a statement.

One practice that I've developed is asking that Divine Source upstairs to guide me. My prayer is often, "Show me the way, Lord." As I said in an earlier journal entry, I like to go through the open doors. Alternatively, if I knock a couple of times and no one answers, I move to another door.

I've seen enough success with this approach that I just keeping looking for that open door. I'm not in control – someone else is.

Wayne Dyer is the author of *Happiness is the Way* and *Change Your Thoughts – Change Your Life*.

Today's Journal

What does it take to look at life this way – as a spiritual being having a human experience?

_____
_____
_____
_____
_____
_____
_____
_____

Describe any meaningful practice that you've undertaken to reflect on life !

_____
_____
_____
_____
_____
_____
_____
_____

Action Step – What will you do with these thoughts? And, by when?

_____
_____
_____

Session 10: Calling

"Everyone has a calling, which is the small, unsettling voice from deep within our souls, an inner urge, which hounds us to live out our purpose in a certain way. A calling is a concern of the spirit. Since a calling implies that someone calls, my belief is that the caller is God."

Dave Wondra

You don't have to be religious to recognize that there's something bigger in this world than merely human existence. That something goes by various names, like Higher Power, Divine Presence, or Ultimate Source.

The quote above comes from Wondra's essay entitled "The Purposeful Prairie" where he uses his wonderings in the Minnesota prairie to clarify his sense of purpose. He argues that like grass in the prairie, we all start from a seed – and that seed has a code embedded in it. Part of that code drives our gifts and talents – those things that bring us joy. That code is different for each of us.

And much like the prairie that moves through a cycle of renewal, so do we. Sometimes we're in Spring when things are blooming, and opportunities are coming our way. Summer is that season when we feel like we're producing, and everything seems fine. But things change just like the seasons and a time of harvesting is upon us.

One of the things that sustains us through change – through those seasons of life – is purpose, or what some people refer to as a calling. When you come to realize that you're not really in control of life's outcomes – just like we're not in control of the seasonal changes – you can explore who or what is in control of those consequences or results.

Sure, you can control your actions – like your words or your schedule – but not the final outcome. Something else is at play. For me, that realization pointed to something outside of myself – what some people call their Higher Power. Most people call that God.

Dave Wondra is the author of *Foundations of Business Communications* and *The Purposeful Prairie*

Today's Journal

Today, what do you feel called to do?

_____

_____

_____

_____

_____

_____

_____

_____

What would hold you back from accepting a Divine call?

_____

_____

_____

_____

_____

_____

_____

_____

Action Step – What will you do with these thoughts? And, by when?

_____

_____

_____

Session 11: Values

"Spirituality is the process of living out a set of deeply held personal values, of honoring a presence greater than ourselves."

Peter Block

That's a big statement. There are a boatload of important values and each person has to choose for himself or herself what's vital versus what sounds good. As you consider what your values are, I'll share some of my values and my process in identifying them.

First and foremost, I think one must have a self-concept best described as a healthy ego. Let's face it – we all have one. Ego plays a role – all the way from a narcissist to a saint. I think a healthy ego is shaped by values like service, compassion and humility. These values cause one to think a bit more about others – to get beyond one's own needs. These are values promoted in the writings of every faith.

One of the best ways to get beyond yourself is to spend some time in solitude – at least in some silence from time-to-time. Give yourself a break to think about what's really important. Be patient with yourself and others. Let the stillness provide guidance.

In my own case, I've benefitted from numerous retreats over the years. I would take two or three days in a remote setting where I could detach from the work-a-day world and be challenged by some big questions. Questions like, "What's really essential right now?" "Who should I be talking to?"

And I've had a love of learning – not in the bookish sense – but rather in being exposed to new things and ideas. I've always had a basic curiosity about how things actually work – especially tools. I just like to exercise my imagination in building things. It is commonly referred to as experiential learning and reflects Einstein's perspective - "There is only one source of wisdom – experience."

Lastly, I value staying healthy. I exercise almost every day and it seems to help me feel energetic and enthused about what's next. And remember, the medical world is pounding away at the importance of exercise for everyone.

Peter Block is the author of *Community – The Structure of Belonging* and *Stewardship*

Today's Journal

What is a process you can use to help you identify your spiritual values?

_____
_____
_____
_____
_____
_____
_____
_____

What are your most important values?

_____
_____
_____
_____
_____
_____
_____
_____

Action Step – What will you do with these thoughts?

_____
_____
_____

Session 12: Gifts

*"We have different gifts, according to the grace given us. If a man's gift
is prophesying, let him use it in proportion to his faith. If it is serving,
let him serve; if it is teaching, let him teach; if it is encouraging, let
him encourage; if it is contributing to the needs of others, let him
give generously; if it is leadership, let him govern diligently."*

The Apostle Paul

The concept here is that a dimension of purposeful living grows out of the premise that you tend to make the greatest contributions when you are engaged in activities that you are good at – that you really enjoy. God created you with specific abilities, instincts, gifts and talents and when you're engaged in them you become energized. This philosophy is often referred at as "positive" or "depth psychology" and is at the other end of the spectrum from an egotistical perspective. It's who you are.

As you identify your key abilities, answer these questions. When do I feel most energetic and fulfilled? What do I really relish? When do I feel a sense of mastery? What aptitude do I share with others, what do they come to me for, that allows mutual satisfaction and growth?

For me, my strengths have served to help me with a purpose of "building a spiritually-oriented community." That entails a lot of enrolling people in various causes and projects. I'm good at generating enthusiasm for these projects. I like designing and building things – sometimes with people – sometimes with wood. I really enjoy facilitating small groups of seekers. Engaging them in the exploration of important questions is really energizing.

I've also really enjoyed writing, even though of the four books I've published, none of them have really taken off. But that's okay, because I wrote them for myself and my family so they knew – beyond any doubt – what I stood for. As I go back and read some of them, I say to myself, "Uh, that's pretty good. You should share that with more people."

Maybe I'll do that !

The **Apostle Paul** was author of *Romans* from which this quote is taken. He also wrote several other books in the **New Testament**.

Today's Journal

What are your gifts, talents and strengths?

_____
_____
_____
_____
_____
_____
_____
_____
_____

On the above attributes, what do you want to put more focus on?

_____
_____
_____
_____
_____
_____
_____
_____

Action Step – What will you do with these thoughts? And, by when?

_____
_____
_____

Session 13: Central Core

*"Purpose is that deepest dimension within us – our central core.
It is the quality we chose to shape our lives around. Purpose
is already within us waiting to be discovered."*

Richard Leider

I appreciate this perspective because it supports the notion that if it's already in us, it must have been put there – sometime – maybe at the very beginning. To me, that signals that it may have come from that Divine Being.

Maybe you could say it was uncovered later in life due to some traumatic event or encounter. And that might be totally valid. Big things usually happen when you have an experience like that. It opens doors that may not have been there – or you just didn't notice them.

Purpose can become clear when we honor silence, as we sit in contemplation, in prayer, or whenever we look deep within. It's a self-discovery process – one that asks you a bunch of important questions – like, "When do I become animated?" Or, "What really gives me delight?"

For me, I found the value I had placed on community had shaped my life. I found the Vail Valley of Colorado had many of the qualities I found interesting. It's relatively small. It's energized by a lot of people that come here, and it's alive with interesting things to do – well beyond skiing. Over time I sharpened my purpose down to "building spiritually-orientated community." It feels so right, but it took many hours of soul-searching. But even with that, it felt like it was waiting to be discovered.

Somewhere along the way I heard Richard Leider say that "Purpose is spiritual wisdom," and I agree with that sentiment – primarily because I believe it comes from deep within us – from that "central core."

Richard Leider is the author of *Something to Live For* and *Work Reimagined*. He is also a co-founder of the **Vail Alliance for Purposeful Living**.

Today's Journal

If you could design your own process to examine your central core, what would it look like?

_____
_____
_____
_____
_____
_____
_____
_____

How would you describe your "central core?"

_____
_____
_____
_____
_____
_____
_____
_____
_____

Action Step – What will you do with these thoughts? And, by when?

_____
_____
_____

Session 14: Calling

"Man's aim in life is not to add to his material possessions, but his predominant calling is to come nearer his Maker."

Mahatma Gandhi

This slight man from India was a powerhouse of thinking and living. His personal possessions could have fit in a bowl or small valise. But his impact around the world was, and is still, something to behold.

"Calling" is another word close to purpose and sometimes it resonates with some people because it seems to come from outside of us – from somewhere out there. To others, a calling comes from inside – deep within our soul. Either way, as Gandhi suggests, we're being asked to come closer to that source. And if that's true, then most people want to discover more about that source.

Drawing near to our maker is pretty central to a meaningful life. It's not the only thing, but just right up there in importance. Most of us call our maker "God," but it's interesting how many other holy names might apply. I like Richard Rohr's tendency to refer to God with some creative descriptors, like Divine Source, Reality Guide, Living Word, Deeper Source, Divine Indwelling, Transcendent Other and Merciful One.

It seems that today's culture is more focused on the material – certainly the things that provide immediate gratification. And there's nothing inherently wrong with those indulgences, but for that to be one's focus is probably limiting. Going deeper into what you're really "called" to do with this one life can be much more satisfying.

And one way to find joy and fulfillment is to understand more about what your Maker has in mind for you. Sitting quietly in contemplation or in prayer and then listening can be very enlightening. What you hear should be considered very carefully. When I hear or sense words or phrases, I get out of bed and write them down.

One night, I got a message from above that said, "go through the open door." My conclusion was to knock on those doors, but if it wasn't answered after a second knock, I'd move on – that was a closed door. It has made life a lot easier !

Mahatma Gandhi was an Indian lawyer, anti-colonial nationalist and political ethicist who employed nonviolent resistance to lead the successful campaign for India's independence from British rule.

Today's Journal

If you want to draw nearer your maker, how would you go about that?

_____

_____

_____

_____

_____

_____

_____

_____

How would you describe your dominate aim in life?

_____

_____

_____

_____

_____

_____

_____

_____

Action Step – What will you do with these thoughts? And, by when?

_____

_____

_____

Session 15: Service

"The greatest leader is seen as servant first because that is what he is deep down inside. Leadership is bestowed on the person who is, by nature, a true servant."

Robert Greenleaf

Serving others is a core spiritual practice. And I'm not talking about waiting on people, but rather helping anyone who is in need. It's an attitude that comes from being other-focused. When someone is engaged this way, others naturally look to them for guidance. It's a very enriching perspective.

What's the difference between a "servant" and a "true servant"? A true servant is one who goes beyond the occasional good deed and lives out of that attitude almost all of the time. It just comes naturally – it's who they are.

For me, it started in the Navy during the Vietnam War, where as a Supply Officer in the Mekong Delta, my job was all about being of service to our troops. The satisfaction of providing what they needed was palpable – you could see it in their faces.

As my career unfolded in Colorado, I had the opportunity to facilitate numerous small groups of up-and-coming leaders. Listening to their stories and helping guide them in examining their directions, I felt I was being of service. Not in the more typical approach of giving advice, but more in asking good questions. Drilling down with follow-up queries like, "Tell me more about that" or "How have you come to that perspective?" My goal was to be supportive so they could answer those questions about service.

I think a true servant is one who is patient with others, always trying to think of things from the other's perspective. Spending adequate time with someone is part of my approach – not being in any hurry to get on to the next subject. People can sense impatience very easily. Just being with them is what a true servant does.

Try it – I believe you'll find satisfaction !

Robert Greenleaf is author of *The Servant as Leader* and *The Power of Servant Leadership*

Today's Journal

When have you felt like serving others? What was that like?

_____
_____
_____
_____
_____
_____
_____
_____

How difficult is it for you to be patient with others?

_____
_____
_____
_____
_____
_____
_____
_____

Action Step – What will you do with these thoughts? And, by when?

_____
_____
_____

Session 16: Action

"This is the true joy in life, the being used for a purpose recognized by yourself as a mighty one; the being thoroughly worn out before you are thrown on the scrap heap; the being a force of nature instead of a feverish, selfish little clod of ailments and grievances complaining that the world will not devote itself to making you happy. I am of the opinion that my life belongs to the whole community, and as long as I live, it is my privilege to do for it whatever I can. I want to be thoroughly used up when I die, for the harder I work, the more I live. I rejoice in life for its own sake. Life is no brief candle to me. It is sort of a splendid torch which I've got a hold of for the moment, and I want to make it burn as brightly as possible before handing it on to future generations."

George Bernard Shaw

This is probably the most profound quote – among many – that I've ever come across. Shaw says so much here that it's hard to even comment on it. But, I'll try !

First, stepping away from normal pace of life, identifying – and then recognizing – your purpose is definitely an important exercise. Being a force for that purpose is for sure a lofty practice. It says you're not going to sit around and hope something happens. No, Shaw is promoting the pro-active life – to stand for something. To take action that makes a difference. To be used up !

For me, I have been strongly influenced by this insightful call. When I first read this, I said to myself, "Get off your butt and move actively on your purpose of "building community." I was inspired by the positive nature of this quote, but I was also reminded to quit complaining about all the hard work ahead of me. My purpose was giving me plenty of reasons to get up in the morning and get about making my community a better place. At seventy-six, I feel like I'm just getting going. In time, to pass this baton to others, I think it will feel like an honor.

But for now, I'm not done !

George Bernard Shaw was an Anglo-Irish playwright, critic, polemicist and political activist. His influence on Western theatre, culture and politics extended from the 1880s to his death and beyond.

Today's Journal

What is your one true joy in life?

_____

_____

_____

_____

_____

_____

_____

_____

How do you manifest this joy?

_____

_____

_____

_____

_____

_____

_____

_____

Action Step – What will you do with these thoughts? And, by when?

_____

_____

_____

Session 17: Dreams

"The future belongs to those who believe in the beauty of their dreams."

Eleanor Roosevelt

Having a dream – or maybe even frequent dreams – is awesome. Giving serious thought to an idea is close to dreaming. Imagining how it might work, who should be involved, and who's going to support that idea, can be a really fun exercise.

As a marketing guy, I was always dreaming. What was our next big program – or next big campaign. When I became chairman of our local Chamber of Commerce, I really started thinking about the larger community. That led to one of life's most common dreams – owning your own home.

In 1978, we built a log home on two acres – calling it the HK Ranch. It was hard because we did much of the laboring ourselves. But as we settled-in, I began to realize our home was simply part of a much larger dream that was taking shape. And then, through a series of personal development workshops, I came to realize that my purpose was to "build community." Over the course of the next two decades, I played an important role in building several community facilities. First, it was an outdoor amphitheater, named after President Gerald Ford. Then it was an indoor performing arts facility, the Vilar Center for the Performing Arts, and lastly, Vail Christian High School.

It was the latter experience that caused me to modify my purpose statement by inserting "spiritually-oriented" between "building" and "community." And from that point on I could see the dream becoming a more robust reality through the formation of multiple small groups of young leaders that helped solidify that community building perspective.

I still believe in the beauty of my dreams. And I'm not done yet. So, pondering – and praying – about what else that dream might include keeps me getting up each morning with expectation.

Thank you, Lord!

Eleanor Roosevelt was an American political figure, diplomat, and activist. She served as the first lady of the United States from 1933 to 1945. She is the author of *The Moral Basis of Democracy* and *It's Up to the Women*.

Today's Journal

Do you have a big dream? If so, describe it !

_____

_____

_____

_____

_____

_____

_____

_____

Describe how you are going about achieving that dream?

_____

_____

_____

_____

_____

_____

_____

_____

Action Step – What will you do with these thoughts? And, by when?

_____

_____

_____

Session 18: Love

*"Love is where we came from, and love is where we are going. When we live in love,
we will not be afraid to die because we have built a bridge between these worlds."*

Richard Rohr

What a beautiful way of looking at life. We're on a bridge between those two worlds of heaven and earth. Between now and then. Between living and dying. And love is the key ingredient in building that bridge.

Rohr is a master at characterizing reality from a mystic's perspective. Love, that feeling of constant affection or connection to another, is central to life, but too many of us can't see it this way. We're too caught-up in the daily pressures and oppressive social media. How do we slow down to smell the roses?

One way for me was coming home to a loving wife and family. We just promoted that feeling and attitude. Being engaged in something around the house, mowing the lawn, raking leaves, building a table, whatever it was, it slowed me down from the day's obligations. Early on, I couldn't see the bridge, but I sensed it was out there somewhere. When I finally clarified my purpose, things started to fall in place.

The bridge helped bring together a philosophy that I called "responsibility linked to surrender." It wasn't one or the other, but both entwined together.

Richard Rohr is the founder of the **Center for Action and Contemplation** and the author of numerous books on spirituality.

Today's Journal

How would you describe the bridge between where you are and where you're going?

_____

_____

_____

_____

_____

_____

_____

_____

How do you view that notion of simply "living in love?"

_____

_____

_____

_____

_____

_____

_____

_____

Action Step – What will you do with these thoughts? And, by when?

_____

_____

_____

Session 19: Vocation

"Vocation is the place where your deepest gladness
and the world's deep hunger meet."

Frederick Bucchner

Vocation is a word that relates to purpose in the broadest sense. So is meaning, calling, mission and other words. In a more narrow reading however, vocation might link-up with a certain skill set, like building, serving or creating. Either way, it's an important concept worth examining.

Then there's the concept called gladness. What does that mean? What's within gladness? For me, gladness has always been linked mostly to the outdoors – to things like skiing, golf, and hiking. But importantly, just being in nature – in God's creation – brings me great joy. Being away from big crowds is very satisfying. Connecting regularly with a small group of like-minded people brings great satisfaction. Obviously, it's different for each individual.

Then we have the question of the world's deep hunger. What is that? I think at a minimum, it's peace, freedom, love and prosperity for everyone. That sounds pretty idealistic – maybe even far-fetched for some. But if one strives to get these diverse forces to meet or merge, then you are doing the best you can. The outcome is in God's hands.

Frederick Bucchner is the author of *Telling the Truth, Sacred Journey* and *Speak What We Feel*

Today's Journal

How would you describe your deepest gladness?

_____

_____

_____

_____

_____

_____

_____

_____

And what about the world's deepest hunger?

_____

_____

_____

_____

_____

_____

_____

Action Step – What will you do with these thoughts? And, by when?

_____

_____

_____

Session 20: Meaning

"Spirituality is a decision to search somewhere other than in findings defined as scientific and their derived practices in secular support systems. Spirituality seeks fundamentally to get beyond material conceptions of meaning."

Peter Vaill

Spirituality can be thought of as a process that takes one inside, into the depths of the soul. It's a process of uncovering what's important to each of us. You can read about the spiritual life or attend seminars and those might be helpful, but the answers to deep questions are usually there buried inside – in your heart.

The purely secular world tends to look for proof – as in facts and statistics. And while information and knowledge will always be valuable, the spiritual realm is different. Rather than hard and fast theories or dogma, the spiritual world allows us to listen and look more for feelings and an intuitive sense that leads to the open door. And all things are possible when we follow God, Buddha, the Universe, your Higher Power, or whoever is your guide as an active force in your life. Stay grounded in your spiritual beliefs and practices.

A spiritually-oriented person understands that we can control our reactions and decisions, but not the outcome of any situation. That is not in our control.

That Divine Source upstairs determines the outcome. Being in communication with him or her can guide your actions and decisions and help you find that meaning that Vaill refers to here.

A spiritual person is usually a good listener !

Peter Vaill is the author of *Spirited Leading and Learning* and *Learning as a Way of Being*

Today's Journal

How does a spiritual perspective help define your significance?

_____
_____
_____
_____
_____
_____
_____
_____

Are you a good listener? If not, why not?

_____
_____
_____
_____
_____
_____
_____
_____

Action Step – What will you do with these thoughts? And, by when?

_____
_____
_____

Session 21: Compassion

"We cannot escape the necessity of love and compassion. This then is my true religion, my simple faith. In this sense, there is no need for temple or church, for mosque or synagogue, no need for complicated philosophy, doctrine or dogma. Our own heart, our mind, is the temple. The doctrine is compassion. Love for others and respect for their rights and dignity, no matter who or what they are. Ultimately, these are all we need."

The Dali Lama

The Dali Lama's philosophy espoused here makes life easier – and makes finding one's purpose easier. When trying to sort out complex situations it's best to keep them as simple as possible.

I suggest that spirituality does not equate to religion, although it's related, but only in a tangential way. As the Dali Lama implies, spirituality is not about church or any particular doctrine. But some religious practices can be very helpful. For example, the process of prayer, of speaking to God, however you relate to that Higher Power, can help you clear your mind. Meditation and contemplation are similar practices that can help quiet down the noise that seems to be all around us these days. In these states, what is important can come to the surface.

De-cluttering your mind can then give you space and time to consider more fundamental questions, like uncovering what your purpose in life might be. To think deeply about what really gives you satisfaction, what makes you come alive, can bring you to what really matters.

And at bottom, isn't compassion part of the foundation of a meaningful life?

The Dali Lama is the author of *The Book of Joy: Lasting Happiness in a Changing World* and *Beyond Religion: Ethics for a Whole World*

Today's Journal

In what ways do you exhibit compassion?

_____
_____
_____
_____
_____
_____
_____
_____

What practices bring you closer to your Maker?

_____
_____
_____
_____
_____
_____
_____
_____

Action Step – What will you do with these thoughts? And, by when?

_____
_____
_____

Session 22: Aliveness

"Don't ask yourself what the world needs. Ask yourself what makes you come alive,
and go do that, because what the world needs is people who have come alive."

Howard Thurman

The world needs a lot of help – no question. You could spend your whole life working on worldly challenges. Think about economic inequality, climate change, pollution, and in early 2020, the pandemic. These are all significant challenges that need to be given their proper attention.

But Thurman approaches those issues from a very different perspective. What if we had tons of people who have come alive for what excites and motivates them? How would that feel if that could be you?

For me, what makes me come alive is the natural environment. Being outside reminds me of how important Mother Nature is in the community-building process. Certainly, people are central to building community, but I've found that connecting with others on a hike or skiing or just sitting on a bench can be very powerful.

While Thurman comes at it from a deep personal perspective, coming alive for something can point toward one's purpose !

Howard Thurman is the author of *For the Inward Journey, The Centering Moment* and *Anchored in the Current*

Today's Journal

What makes you come alive?

_____

_____

_____

_____

_____

_____

_____

_____

How can the world benefit from that thing that makes you come alive?

_____

_____

_____

_____

_____

_____

_____

_____

Action Step – What will you do with these thoughts? And, by when?

_____

_____

_____

Session 23: Possibilities

*"The thing that stands between man and what he wants from life is
often merely the will to try it and the faith to believe it is possible."*

Richard DeVos

Richard DeVos was a man who believed anything was possible. He was the co-founder of Amway, the giant multi-level marketing firm, who gave away much of his wealth.

What one wants from life is not always the first thing that comes to mind when pondering the possible. But by taking a thoughtful, careful examination of what's really significant, what inspires you, some interesting conclusions and ideas can present themselves. When you recognize your most important values and your most important assets, a picture of what might be possible often appears.

Then, stepping out and giving some things a try, often reveals those new possibilities. Maybe you'll find that thing you think is a perfect fit. Or alternatively, you discover it's not for you. But the willingness to try, the trusting that nothing tried will always end in nothing gained. Being a person who is willing to explore will almost always result in something learned.

It's the trying that makes the difference.

Richard DeVos is the author of *All the Light We Cannot See* and *Compassionate Capitalism: People Helping People Help Themselves.*

Today's Journal

What have you recently tried that surprised you?

_____
_____
_____
_____
_____
_____
_____
_____

What aspects of that exploration were a bust, and hopefully, resulted in a lesson learned?

_____
_____
_____
_____
_____
_____
_____
_____

Action Steps – What will you do with these thoughts? And, by when?

_____
_____
_____

Session 24: Wisdom

This is one of the goals of the Jewish way of living: to experience commonplace deeds as spiritual adventures, to feel the hidden love and wisdom in all things.

Abraham Joshua Heschel

What a wonderful way of thinking. To go to the grocery store as a spiritual adventure. Who might you see? To take out the trash and bump into a neighbor and have a spontaneous conversation about something beyond the weather. How cool is that?

Too often, many of us get caught-up in the pressures of the day or some frustrating social media post that gets us all worked-up. These things are real, no doubt. But what if we could just let them go and concentrate on what's at hand – what's right in front of us. The pop psychologists might call this "being in the moment."

The ability to be present, to find the hidden love in everyday occurrences, takes time and maturity. Or as Rabbi Heschel implies, comes from the attainment of wisdom. This approach is realistic and yet hopeful. Let your experience be the major influence in your life !

Abraham Joshua Heschel was a Polish-born American rabbi and one of the leading Jewish theologians and Jewish philosophers of the 20th century.

Today's Journal

How do you experience the commonplace?

_____
_____
_____
_____
_____
_____
_____
_____

How have you attained the level of wisdom you think you have?

_____
_____
_____
_____
_____
_____
_____
_____

Action Steps – What will you do with these thoughts? And, by when?

_____
_____
_____

Session 25: Passions

*"Passions give life meaning, and it is through passionate commitment
that we give our lives the particular meaning that they have."*

Tom Rollins

Understanding – deeply understanding – your passions can be very revealing. Spend a few minutes thinking about what those passions tend to be. Do they involve athletics, or the outdoors, or music? What are those things?

Then, think about how committed you are to those passions. Are they occasional practices or do you devote significant time to them? Of those passions you identified, what's most important?

For me, an important passion is working in various ways to build community. Whether it's in small groups of 5-6, or helping a vital non-profit, just connecting with friends, the opportunity to be in relationship with elements of my community is very satisfying.

Another passion is writing. While I've published several books, my interest was never in making any money, but rather recording my thinking, and then, years later, referring back to what I've recorded and finding it very interesting that that is still how I feel about whatever the focus was.

Lastly, for me reading is a passion – particularly history. I really enjoy being reminded of all the good things – and some not so good – that have transpired over the years. Continuing to learn has always been interesting to me.

If you're not spending significant time engaged in your passions, it's time to reevaluate your priorities.

Tom Rollins is the author of *Under One Flag* and *The 100 Greatest Ideas of All Time.*

Today's Journal

What are your passions?

_____

_____

_____

_____

_____

_____

_____

_____

How committed are you to each of those passions?

_____

_____

_____

_____

_____

_____

_____

_____

Action Steps – What will you do with these thoughts? And, by when?

_____

_____

_____

Session 26: Voice

"Vocation does not come from a voice "out there" calling me to become something I am not. It comes from a voice "in here" calling me to be the person I was born to be, to fulfill the original selfhood given me at birth by God."

Parker Palmer

Vocation is related to purpose in that, even though it often applies to our jobs or professions, it supports that larger calling – at least it should. Vocation in this more traditional sense can come from somewhere "out there," especially if you haven't taken the time to look "in here."

For many people, listening to that internal voice doesn't come naturally. Our lives are often so hectic there's very little time to just sit and contemplate and take a walk in nature. But finding that time can pay significant benefits. Get away from all those normal distractions and just listen. Of course, this assumes there's a "caller," a place or a person or that Higher Power, that Mystical Presence, that we all hear about.

For me, that caller spoke ever so clearly one night – I don't remember the exact date – but it was crystal clear. Even though I mentioned this in an earlier chapter, an inner voice spoke saying, "Declare your faith – stay the course."

"Declare" meant to walk my talk, to express what I stand for, more through my actions than any prescribed set of words. "Stay" meant to remain in my small town and keep doing the work of building community. Sometimes that's building relationships and sometimes it's building facilities.

And I keep looking for those open doors. I really think that's what I was called to do !

Parker Palmer is the author of *Let Your Life Speak, A Hidden Wholeness* and *To Know As We Are Known.* He is also the founder of the **Center for Courage & Renewal**

Today's Journal

Have you ever heard from that inner voice? If so, what was that?

_____
_____
_____
_____
_____
_____
_____
_____
_____

When you experience a closed door, what do you do?

_____
_____
_____
_____
_____
_____
_____
_____
_____

Action Steps – What will you do with these thoughts? And, by when?

_____
_____
_____

Session 27: Success

"We may spend our whole life climbing the ladder of success, only to discover that, when we got to the top, our ladder is leaning against the wrong wall."

Thomas Merton

Climbing a corporate ladder is pretty typical – I certainly did – for a long time. And while there's not much wrong with seeking success, Merton is challenging us to think deeply about just what we're striving for.

Finding the right wall is not necessarily easy. Oft times we fall into a career without much thought. Sometimes it's the first thing that comes along – or after searching for months, we just take the first pathway offered because we needed the money. That, of course, is the short-term approach, but it gets us started. Finding the right long-term path however takes time, patience, and perhaps a little guidance and reflection.

Discovering that right wall starts with examining what's at the core of who you are and who you want to become. It starts by answering those classic questions repeated from earlier pages in this journal. What do you really value? What makes you come alive? What do you lose yourself in? What are your passions and why do you get up in the morning?

But just answering these questions is not usually enough. One of the best ways to flesh-out your interests is to get with a small group of trusted peers. Maybe it's a men's group, or people from organizations in the same industry – although you should avoid direct competitors. Talk out what you've discovered. Allow your peers to probe your answers from what they perceive about you. Carefully listen to their opinions and then go somewhere quiet and think about what you've written and heard. Then do it again until you hear guidance from above.

Thomas Merton is the author of *The Way of Chuang Tzu* and *The Seven Storey Mountain*

Today's Journal

How would you describe the wall your ladder is leaning against right now?

_____

_____

_____

_____

_____

_____

_____

_____

Does that feel right? If not, describe what feels off for you?

_____

_____

_____

_____

_____

_____

_____

_____

Action Steps – What will you do with these thoughts? And, by when?

_____

_____

_____

Session 28: Perseverance

"The important thing in life is to have a great aim and to possess the aptitude and perseverance to attain it."

Johann Goethe

Having a great aim is an aspect of purpose in that it points to an important goal. And both an aim and goals – even objectives – will yield greater clarity when directed toward some purpose.

Goethe's comment here speaks to how to obtain those kinds of important things. Aptitude is often developed in some kind of educational or learning context – but not always. Sometimes an aptitude or a skill is just naturally inherent. But getting a good education builds a foundation upon which to grow. I think life-long learning of almost any variety keeps us exploring and interested. Reading quality magazines and books keeps us stretching and discovering – so to do seminars, retreats, and intensive classes. The possibilities are endless in the online world.

And the perseverance aspect is also critical. One dimension of this is keeping your commitments, those things you've promised yourself or to someone else. Perseverance is about sticking with that project or idea you've been kicking around. It requires patience. It's about not giving up. Going about a process like this – or almost any thoughtful exercise – can lead you toward your purpose. But keep in mind that your purpose will generally evolve over time – it's more a process than simply an aim that doesn't change !

Johann Goethe is the author of *Maxims and Reflections* and *Wilhelm Meister's Apprenticeship*

Today's Journal

What is your great aim in life?

_____

_____

_____

_____

_____

_____

_____

_____

Are you sticking with that? If so, where is that taking you?

_____

_____

_____

_____

_____

_____

_____

_____

Action Steps – What will you do with these thoughts? And, by when?

_____

_____

_____

Session 29: Direction

"Don't go where the path may lead; go instead where there is no path and leave a trail."

Ralph Waldo Emerson

Emerson was prolific as a poet, author and essayist in the mid-1800's. His thinking was broadly admired and his influence was wide spread.

This quote about choosing a path is indicative of his thought processes. Rather than go where everyone else has gone, he's saying choose you own route. Taking a well-worn path can often be easier as many others have gone that way. It's a path that is usually well-marked with guidance along the way. It's probably safer than striking out on your own.

But leaving a trail is an approach for adventurers and entrepreneurs. This method is for inquisitive and creative types who want to carve out a new way of doing things. It may not always produce the result hoped for, but it leaves a trail that others may benefit from. Breaking away from the normal method or tactic may reflect how one views his or her purpose. Even when generally not visible, fostering a new trail is often what an experienced leader does.

And it most often comes from a person who knows what he or she is here to do. It's a person who is clear about purpose and life direction.

Ralph Waldo Emerson is the author of *The Conduct of Life, Nature* and *Society and Solitude*

Today's Journal

Have you ever blazed a trail?

_____

_____

_____

_____

_____

_____

_____

_____

If you don't consider yourself an explorer, what attribute best describes you?

_____

_____

_____

_____

_____

_____

_____

_____

Action Step – What will you do with these thoughts? And, by when?

_____

_____

_____

Session 30: Meaning

"Meaning is not something that you stumble across, like the answer to a riddle or the prize in a treasure hunt. Meaning is something you build into your life. You build it out of your own past, out of your affections and loyalties, out of the experience of humankind as it is passed on to you, out of your own talent and understanding, out of the things you believe in, out of the things and people you love, out of the values for which you are willing to sacrifice something. The ingredients are there. You are the only one who can put them together into that unique pattern that will be your life. Let it be a life that has dignity and meaning for you"

John Gardner

As Gardner advocates here, meaning is not a fluke or happenstance occurrence. It's rare that something this important will just fall into your lab. No, it takes thought and introspection – and time. Most people have to work at it. It's not necessarily hard work, but it takes a willingness to be fully honest with yourself. For some people, prayer or meditation helps.

Finding what "meaning" is for you is more an uncovering than anything else. It's bound-up in your values, your beliefs, your passions, and your life experiences thus far. As Gardner says, the ingredients or elements are already there. As you articulate those elements, either in writing or in conversation with a mentor or a small group of trusted friends, what's important, and why that's important, can create clarity.

Meaning is an individual thing. It's distinctive to you. Some standard line like, "I'm here to change the world," is too general and too common. No, your purpose comes out of those attributes and longings that you've identified for yourself – what you've built into your life thus far, and those dreams you've yet to realize.

Spend time with these questions and something will result – guaranteed – well, almost !

John Gardner is the author of *The Sunlight Dialogues* and *On Moral Fiction*

Today's Journal

What personal attributes do you hold most dear?

_____

_____

_____

_____

_____

_____

_____

_____

_____

What processes or exercises do you use to uncover answers to difficult questions?

_____

_____

_____

_____

_____

_____

_____

_____

Action Step – What will you do with these thoughts? And, by when?

_____

_____

_____

Session 31: Know Thyself

"If we could first know where we are, and whither we are tending,
we could better judge what to do, and how to do it."

Abraham Lincoln

Lincoln may not have meant it, but he was restating what that famous Greek philosopher, **Socrates** declared, "that the unexamined life was not worth living." Asked to sum up what all philosophical commandments could be reduced to, he replied: "Know thyself." Knowing yourself has extraordinary prestige and great value in today's culture.

Knowing where we are is not a primarily geographic issue, it's asking where we are in life? Are you just starting out or have you embarked on an initial vocation or mission? Are you in midlife with a new family and growing responsibilities? What is your faith perspective and are you practicing some traditions passed down to you through your family? Understanding, examining where you stand is a prerequisite to moving forward.

And then knowing in which direction you are headed is just as important. Having a vision of what a desired future looks like does not come automatically – or out of thin air. No, you must work at, you must spend time in quiet solitude, taking your life experiences into consideration. And most importantly, that vision will be more meaningful when it evolves from a clear sense of purpose

Having a purpose and vision in place will give direction of what you need to do and how to do it. Lincoln saw this long before modern-day psychologists and mystics created an industry to examine these issues.

Abraham Lincoln was the 16th President of the United States and he was the author of the *Gettysburg Address* and *Meditation on the Divine Will.*

Today's Journal

How would you describe where you are in life today?

_____

_____

_____

_____

_____

_____

_____

_____

And whither are you tending?

_____

_____

_____

_____

_____

_____

_____

_____

Action Step – What will you do with these thoughts? And, by when?

_____

_____

_____

Session 32: Service

*"Everyone must work to live, but the purpose of life is to serve
and to show compassion and the will to help others."*

Albert Schweitzer

Dr. Schweitzer certainly has the reputation to make this claim. His experience in Africa with the poor and indigent pointed him in this direction of serving and helping others. Perhaps his expression here is really a statement regarding his own personal purpose. He was clearly a servant leader.

Without diminishing his purpose, it's important to recognize that "the purpose of life" is particular to each individual. While serving and showing compassion are hugely important, they are not the only way one can direct his or her life.

For example, my own purpose revolves around the notion of building. It started when I was quite young building a cabinet for my mother's stereo equipment. During college it morphed into building friendships with my Delta Chi fraternity brothers. In the Navy, it became strengthening and fortifying my team aboard the USS Jennings County in the Mekong River. Later, my wife and I built our own log home in Colorado's Lake Creek Valley. And then I led a team of people in building the Vail Leadership Institute, an organization whose mission was to help shape our community.

When I decided to expand the spiritual dimension of my life, serving others in my community became much more important. And because purpose evolves, I've actually toyed with the thought of replacing "building" with "serving."

It differs from Dr. Schweitzer's wonderful example, and it shows that purpose can be expressed in many ways.

Albert Schweitzer is the author of *Answering the Call, Out of My Life* and *Thought and The Light Within Us*

Today's Journal

How has your purpose evolved over time?

_____

_____

_____

_____

_____

_____

_____

_____

How are you living out that perspective?

_____

_____

_____

_____

_____

_____

_____

_____

Action Step – What will you do with these thoughts? And, by when?

_____

_____

_____

Session 33: Heart

"I use the word heart as they did in ancient times, when it didn't merely mean the emotions, as it tends to mean today. It meant that center in the human self where everything comes together – where will and intellect and values and feeling and intuition and vision all converge. It meant the source of one's integrity. It takes courage to lead from the heart."

Parker Palmer

Palmer's definition of heart is wonderfully comprehensive. It implies that the power of the spiritual can bring many diverse elements together. Spirituality helps cause integration – where everything comes together.

As I mentioned in an earlier Session, Matthew 23:26 inspired me to develop a curriculum around the notion of working on the heart before taking on all the head attributes. It gave birth to a philosophy we labelled "Inside First™." This expression resonates with Palmer's reference here to the heart.

Effective, ethical leaders need to draw upon both head and heart. The concept of integration makes sense when you recognize that God gave us free will to choose, and yet he reminds us periodically, that he's got a plan too.

The integration of opposite dimensions, the analytical with the creative, the strategic with the visionary, action blended with patience, competence with character, can become a potent purposeful living process. But in the final analysis, if you find conflict between these extremes, follow your heart.

Parker Palmer is an author, educator, and activist who focuses on issues in education, community, leadership, spirituality, and social change. He is the founder and Senior Partner Emeritus of the **Center for Courage and Renewal.**

Today's Journal

What does it mean to you to lead from the heart?

_____

_____

_____

_____

_____

_____

_____

_____

Describe a situation where you found your head and heart in conflict?

_____

_____

_____

_____

_____

_____

_____

_____

Action Step – What will you do with these thoughts? And, by when?

_____

_____

_____

Session 34: Solitude

*"They will forget the rush and strain of all the other weeks of the year, and for
a short time at least, the days will be good for their bodies and good for their
souls. Once more they will lay hold of the perspective that comes to those who
every morning and every night can lift their eyes up to Mother Nature."*

Theodore Roosevelt

TR understood the power of the natural environment. His legacy includes the many national parks and forests that his passion helped create. He knew through his own experience that nature was inspiring but needed protection.

In today's globalized and digitized world, nature can provide a wonderful tonic from the "rush and strain." It can provide a place to reflect, to weigh the decisions awaiting you at the office or at home. It can help you focus on what's really important.

In the solitude of nature, you can find rejuvenation – maybe even transformation. You can see the cycles of renewal in the seasons. You see the hand of Mother Nature and the perfection she has created. At every opportunity, seek solitude for it might just provide a spiritual path to purpose.

Theodore Roosevelt was the 26th President of the United States. He is the author of *The River of Doubt* and *The Naturalist*.

Today's Journal

When has solitude been helpful to you? Describe a situation that really moved you?

_____
_____
_____
_____
_____
_____
_____
_____
_____

What resulted from this experience?

_____
_____
_____
_____
_____
_____
_____
_____
_____

Action Step – What will you do with these thoughts? And, by when?

_____
_____
_____

Session 35: Conversation

"God is having one conversation with humankind, but in a thousand voices. Religious people all over the world need to be in conversation with each other so that we understand the fullness of God's conversation with us. The complete story of God is discovered in how the sacred manifests in every religion, in every gesture a person makes toward the Divine."

Rick Fabian

There are many ways to hear from God. Those with a strongly held doctrine would say there's only one way. These are the same people who strive to make certain that which is essentially a mystery.

One of the largest responsibilities of a leader is to create understanding among the people in the organization. How do effective leaders do this? One of the best ways is to foster conversations – to pose questions that provoke thoughtful interactions – and to listen – and to acknowledge the contributions and perspectives of others. Listen to understand – not to respond. The principles of dialogue can really help here. This approach brings out divergent perspectives and new ideas.

When you realize that not everyone thinks just like you, and that you don't have all the answers, you can grow as a person. This growth comes from respecting, really honoring, views other than your own. This approach creates understanding and understanding leads to harmony.

Rick Fabian is the author of *Signs of Life*. He began to develop his unique approach to Christian spirituality while he served as chaplain to the **Episcopal Church at Yale**.

Today's Journal

How do you react to those who see things differently?

_____
_____
_____
_____
_____
_____
_____
_____

When was the last time you had a robust conversation with a friend or colleague? What was that like?

_____
_____
_____
_____
_____
_____
_____
_____

Action Step – What will you do with these thoughts? And, by when?

_____
_____
_____

Session 36: Joy

*"When seeking your purpose, ask these questions. Does it fit
your values? Does it evoke excellence? And does it bring you
that subjective barometer of engagement – joy?"*

Howard Gardner

These are excellent questions. And you could add things like what are your aptitudes, what are your desires and what do you find really engaging?

By exploring these types of questions and being really honest about your answers, you can begin to zero-in on that all important purpose statement. That barometer of joy may be the most significant because that's a state that we all want to be in. What does that look like for you?

For me, joy comes from building things – sometimes it's tables or some furniture that improves our log home. Sometimes it's simply riding my mountain bike and listening to inspiring music. Other times, it's just sitting in front of the fireplace with a good book. And then there's cementing relationships with friends through engaged conversation.

For me, all of this relates to my evolving purpose of "serving spiritually-oriented community."

Howard Gardner is the author of *Multiple Intelligences, The Unschooled Mind* and *Changing Minds.* He is a Professor of Cognition and Education at the Graduate School of Education at **Harvard University**.

Today's Journal

What activities evoke joy in you?

_____

_____

_____

_____

_____

_____

_____

_____

How much time do you really spend in these joyful undertakings?

_____

_____

_____

_____

_____

_____

_____

_____

Action Step – What will you do with these thoughts? And, by when?

_____

_____

_____

Session 37: Liberation

"Our deepest fear is not that we are inadequate. Our deepest fear is that we are powerful beyond measure. It is our light, not our darkness, that most frightens us. We ask ourselves, who am I to be brilliant, gorgeous, talented and fabulous? Actually, who are you <u>not</u> to be? You are a child of God. Your playing small doesn't serve the world. There is nothing enlightened about shrinking so that other people won't feel insecure around you. We are all meant to shine. It is not just in some of us, it's in everyone. And as we let our own light shine, we unconsciously give other people permission to do the same. As we are liberated from our own fear, our presence automatically liberates others."

Marianne Williamson

What a powerful message. Are you *not* brilliant and fabulous and those other attributes? Of course you are. So, in what areas *are* you brilliant?

In order to take Williamson's positive approach, you need to assess your gifts and endowments. As I've said earlier, you ought to develop those things you're really good at. Take a course or seminar, study books and become more and more familiar with those areas of interest that call you. Become an expert on those things – whatever they are.

When you combine your thoughts on abilities with other cravings and interests, you're building the components of a meaningful purpose. And when you're passionate about something, others get it. They see your hunger and are inspired by your attitude. They almost always want that same energy in their own thinking.

So don't hold back. Be enthused about living that purposeful life !

Marianne Williamson is the author of *Age of Miracles, When Things Fall Apart* and *A Course in Miracles.*

Today's Journal

When was a time in your life that you felt liberated?

_____

_____

_____

_____

_____

_____

_____

_____

What are the conditions for you when you really shine?

_____

_____

_____

_____

_____

_____

_____

Action Step – What will you do with these thoughts? And, by when?

_____

_____

_____

Session 38: Spirituality

"Spirituality fosters character development, love, compassion and a sense of responsibility."

Jay Sidhu

This quote says it all – or almost all – that one needs to understand and master in achieving the good life.

Having said that, character development does not come automatically or easily. It's really a lifelong process of learning from your mistakes and seeing what actually works in the real world, but most importantly in relationships. How you treat people, how you keep your agreements, how you communicate, and how you collaborate signals the kind of person you are.

Love and compassion are attributes that usually win the day. In this case, the word love is not referring to the romantic variety, but rather the caring we show to others. Are we truly interested in helping other people – being of service to someone in need? And compassion is no more than the demonstration of empathy and kindness for others. It's not that hard when you are able to shift your focus away from your own selfish desires. This is how you exhibit a healthy ego.

To me, a sense of responsibility is key to evolving one's character. To take responsibility for just about anything says that you are someone who cares – who's engaged. And, as stated earlier, a responsible person recognizes that he or she can't control the outcome. That's when surrender comes into play.

Delivering on your commitments says you can be counted on. And when you deliver with a sense of love and compassion, people will beat a path to your door.

Jay Sidhu is the author of *Embracing Defeat: Japan in the Wake of World War II.*

Today's Journal

What does character development involve for you?

_____

_____

_____

_____

_____

_____

_____

_____

Describe how you view responsibility.

_____

_____

_____

_____

_____

_____

_____

_____

Action Step – What will you do with these thoughts? And, by when?

_____

_____

_____

Session 39: Integration

"We are explorers and the most compelling frontier of our time is human consciousness. Our quest is the integration of science and spirituality, a vision which reminds us of our connectedness to the inner self, to each other, and to the earth."

Edgar Mitchell

It is obvious that Edgar Mitchell was much more than an astronaut because going into outer space most certainly gives one a broader perspective on life. And integrating science and spirituality definitely calls upon a "both/and" outlook, a non-dualistic attitude.

By blending these two polar opposite concepts, it can point one toward a more beautiful world. There is no doubt that scientific discoveries have changed the world, mostly for the better. Think of the advancements in medicine, in manufacturing, in technology – it's amazing what we now enjoy because of man's use of knowledge.

Spirituality is a softer, less precise understanding of the way we work in the world. It relates to the soul, as opposed to material or physical things, and often includes a sense of connection to something greater than ourselves. Incorporating a Divine Presence into one's life can be a powerful way to seek meaning and significance over self-aggrandizement. Many people believe that character and ethics can be built on and enriched by a spiritual perspective. Engaging in spiritual dialogue offers the opportunity for understanding a deeper sense of self.

Fusing these concepts, as Mitchell advocates, can keep us connected to what's really important, especially to each other.

Edgar Dean Mitchell was a United States Navy officer and aviator, test pilot, aeronautical engineer, and a NASA astronaut. As the Lunar Module Pilot of Apollo 14, he spent nine hours working on the lunar surface

Today's Journal

What does the description "Divine Presence" mean to you?

_____

_____

_____

_____

_____

_____

_____

_____

What's your sense of how well our culture has integrated science and spirituality?

_____

_____

_____

_____

_____

_____

_____

_____

_____

Action Step – What will you do with these thoughts? And, by when?

_____

_____

_____

Session 40: Creativity

"Personal mastery means approaching one's life as a creative work,
living life from a creative as opposed to reactive viewpoint."

Peter Senge

What Senge is implying here is that you have a responsibility to build your life around some meaningful purpose. When you delve down into the purpose-building process, you find that it can be a pretty creative undertaking.

The creative activity tends to ask a lot of good questions; like many of those here in previous sessions. When you really think about what you lose yourself in, you start to remember those instances when you were completely consumed by some thing, or some person. For me, it was being outdoors – out in Colorado's natural environment. What I saw and what excited me was how beautiful Mother Nature could be.

The reactive viewpoint is very different. It tends to be an unthinking approach – you just respond automatically, not giving much thought to what you're doing or where that action might be taking you. Taking the alternative route – looking at your life as a creative work – is much more interesting, if not fascinating.

Determining where you want to go – creating a significant purpose – moves one toward personal mastery.

Peter Senge is the author of *The Fifth Discipline* and *The Necessary Revolution*

Today's Journal

In what areas of your life do you feel creative?

_____

_____

_____

_____

_____

_____

_____

_____

Describe a time when you simply reacted to your situation?

_____

_____

_____

_____

_____

_____

_____

_____

Action Step – What will you do with these thoughts? And, by when?

_____

_____

_____

Session 41: Attitude

"Attitude is not fully conditioned and determined; he determines himself whether to give in to conditions or to stand up to them. In other words, man is ultimately self-determining. Man does not simply exist, but always decides what his existence will be, what he will become in the next moment."

Viktor Frankl

Given that Frankl developed this perspective while in a German concentration camp during World War II, it's amazing that his attitude could be so positive. In his book, **Man's Search for Meani**ng, he advocates that our most fundamental freedom is the ability to choose.

Self-determination is a good way of describing how one can obtain a clear purpose for one's life. You're in charge of what you will become – moment by moment – even though you're not in control of the outcome. That's God's domain. One way of managing the complexity of control is to go through the open doors. You might bang on closed doors now and then but going through the open ones is easier.

If you can maintain an optimistic outlook – a positive attitude – going through those open doors, you will have chosen well. If you can articulate a meaningful purpose and periodically evaluate how you're doing against that purpose, you will be living a self-determined life. If you choose to do that through a spiritual lens, you will be on a very good path.

Viktor Emil Frankl was an Austrian neurologist, psychiatrist, philosopher, author, and Holocaust survivor. He was the founder of logotherapy, a school of psychotherapy which describes a search for a life meaning as the central human motivational force.

Today's Journal

What is a difficult choice you've had to make that turned out well?

_____

_____

_____

_____

_____

_____

_____

_____

_____

What about a decision that didn't turn out so well? What was that like?

_____

_____

_____

_____

_____

_____

_____

_____

Action Step – What will you do with these thoughts? And, by when?

_____

_____

_____

Session 42: Silence

"Silence provides a deep insight into reality, a capacity to see beneath the surface of nature and people, an awareness that uncovers for us a spiritual vitality in our world, in ourselves - and points us toward God."

Don Postema

Silence is a rarity in today's culture but is needed more than ever. When silence helps us achieve spiritual vitality it becomes a true blessing. Silence allows us to think and dream and envision a desired future.

As we think about that future, the question of purpose ought to come into focus – if not examination. Coming back to your purpose statement periodically – like annually – is an excellent way to help you stay on the track that your vision anticipates.

And time in silent meditation allows you to hear more clearly from that Divine Presence. When you hear that voice, however clear it might be – you should really pay attention – in fact, stop doing whatever you're up to and write that down.

That's happened to me more than once and reviewing those notes has been very instructive. It influenced me greatly such that it helped confirm my purpose.

Silence is not devoid of action – it points us toward God.

Don Postema is the author of *Space for God: A Leader's Guide to the Study and Practice of Spirituality and Prayer* and *Catch Your Breath: God's Invitation to Sabbath Rest*

Today's Journal

Describe a time when silence was helpful?

_____

_____

_____

_____

_____

_____

_____

_____

If you have a meditation practice, describe that here !

_____

_____

_____

_____

_____

_____

_____

_____

Action Step – What will you do with these thoughts? And, by when?

_____

_____

_____

Session 43: Control

"If God told you exactly what it was you were to do, you would be happy doing it no matter what it was. What you're doing is what God wants you to do. Be happy."

Werner Erhard

In the late 60's, Werner Erhard created a program call est that stood for Erhard Seminars Training. It was radical and transforming because it challenged me to think about what I was doing and who I was becoming.

If you believe in God, regardless of what label you assign to that Higher Power or Supreme Being, you know he, or she, is in ultimate control. You can direct your actions, but you aren't really in control of the end result — of the consequence. Letting go of wanting to control the conclusion — expecting to direct the outcomes — is pretty difficult for almost everyone. Believers tend to think that what they're doing is what God wants them to do.

Another oft-repeated Erhard line was "be here now." You can't be anywhere other than where you are so why focus on what has happened in the past or what might happen in the future? Living life in the moment is sometimes hard, but if you're smelling the roses, you're doing what God wants of you.

Be happy !

Werner Hans Erhard is an American lecturer known for founding **Erhard Seminars Training** which operated from 1971 to 1984. He has written, lectured, and taught on self-improvement. The program is now called the **Landmark Forum**.

Today's Journal

Are you doing what God wants you to do? If not, why not?

_____

_____

_____

_____

_____

_____

_____

_____

How often can you live in the "be here now" moment? What gets in your way?

_____

_____

_____

_____

_____

_____

_____

_____

Action Step – What will you do with these thoughts? And, by when?

_____

_____

_____

Session 44: Inner Voice

"Your time is limited, so don't waste it living someone else's life. Don't be trapped by dogma, which is living with the results of other people's thinking. Don't let the noise of others' opinions drown out your own inner voice. And most importantly, have the courage to follow your heart and intuition."

Steve Jobs

In today's fast paced, media-driven world, it's very difficult to not be influenced by what other people are saying and doing. Headlines grab our attention at all hours and negative news is what sells. Steve Jobs, known more for his technological advances, obviously has a spiritual side as well.

While it's astute to listen to other's opinions and gain wider understanding, Jobs encourages us to also listen to our own inner voice – which many people say is the Holy Spirit. When I get those prompts, I write then down immediately. Like when I heard "stay the course" and then spent hours, if not days, trying to apply that to my current situation. I knew straight away it was God advising me of an important course. I was being directed to keep doing what I was doing.

Having the courage to follow your heart takes a mature worldview. It requires trusting that the Creator has your best interests in mind. It necessitates surrendering to something beyond yourself. It requires courage to recognize that you are not in control.

And that's not easy !

Steven Paul Jobs was an American business magnate, founder of **Apple Computers**, industrial designer, investor, and media proprietor. He is also the author of *The Life, Lessons & Rules for Success.*

Today's Journal

What is your inner voice calling you to do?

_____

_____

_____

_____

_____

_____

_____

_____

When have you felt courageous?

_____

_____

_____

_____

_____

_____

_____

_____

Action Step – What will you do with these thoughts? And, by when?

_____

_____

_____

Session 45: Influence

"Do you want to be a positive influence in the world? First, get your own life in order. Ground yourself in the single principle so that your behavior is wholesome and effective. If you do that, you will earn respect and powerful influence. Your behavior influences others through a ripple effect. A ripple effect works because everyone influences everyone else. Powerful people are powerful influences. If your life works, you influence your family. If your family works, your family influences your community. If your community works, your community influences the nation. If your nation works, your nation influences your world."

John Heider

While Heider doesn't specify what that "single principle" is, I believe he's referring to purpose, because in my experience, that is the one concept that has the kind of influence he refers to. A positive and clear purpose that is consistently pursued will almost always lead to that wholesome and effective behavior.

The ripple effect outlined here can be a potent influence – it can change the world – and it starts at home. You don't have to create a new organization, you don't have to get a Ph.D., and you don't have to solve world hunger. By focusing on those people nearest, by really being with them, you can influence their conduct. When people see how you treat others they don't need to be told how to behave – they grasp it. Your action is so much more powerful than any words you might offer.

Your influence ripples out way beyond what you perceive. Live a purposeful life and watch the world get better !

John Heider is the author of *The Tao of Leadership*.

Today's Journal

In what ways do you feel you have influence?

_____
_____
_____
_____
_____
_____
_____
_____

Right behind purpose, what is the next most important principle in your life?

_____
_____
_____
_____
_____
_____
_____
_____

Action Step – What will you do with these thoughts? And, by when?

_____
_____
_____

Session 46: Vision

"Your vision will become clear only when you look into your heart.
Who looks outside, dreams; who looks inside, awakens."

Carl Jung

Visioning can be a very powerful exercise, especially if you do it frequently – like annually, or even more often. Jung suggests the importance of a deep, meditative experience.

Dreaming is okay, but it has its limits. Envisioning what your future might look like can be helpful as long as it doesn't get into fantasizing or hallucinating. Journaling these thoughts and ideas can become influences as you craft or revise your purpose.

The key to creating a vision from your ideas, and other factors like values and strengths, is to examine your heart. What is at the deepest reaches of your soul? What's really essential to you? Looking inside doesn't come naturally to most of us. Meditation or contemplative prayer can help. Getting away, taking a retreat or finding a solitary place can be important.

When you do any of these things there's a good chance that you will awaken to your passions. If you're listening carefully, you may even hear a suggestion from above. A new calling may evolve. Something good is likely to happen

Carl Gustav Jung was a Swiss psychiatrist and psychoanalyst who founded analytical psychology. Jung's work has been influential in the fields of psychiatry, anthropology, archaeology, literature, philosophy, psychology and religious studies. He was the author of *Memories, Dreams and Reflections, The Undiscovered Self: The Dilemma of the Individual in Modern Society.*

Today's Journal

How would you articulate a vision for your life?

_____

_____

_____

_____

_____

_____

_____

_____

What practices do you use to look inside?

_____

_____

_____

_____

_____

_____

_____

_____

Action Step – What will you do with these thoughts? And, by when?

_____

_____

_____

Session 47: Direction

"I find the great thing in this world is not where we stand, but in what direction we are moving."

Oliver Wendall Holmes

Where you stand and what you stand for is vitally important. It speaks to who you are as a person and what people can count on you for. The values and principles that make-up your character create a solid foundation upon which to stand. These are all good things.

The question Holmes is alluding to here is what are you doing with all of that? Having a clear purpose and a vision for your future can help signal that direction. But even these statements may not be enough. What are you doing today, this week, this year to advance that future? Do you have a plan? Is it written down? Do you review it periodically?

One approach I've used over the years is called my "annual look" where I go away, sometimes on a retreat, or sometimes just in the backyard. The key is to find some solitude where I can just "be." I find a time of contemplative prayer helps. And it's more listening than praying out loud. For me, it's a spiritual path of purpose.

Oliver Wendall Holmes, Jr. has been called the greatest jurist and legal scholar in the history of the English-speaking world. He is the author of *The Essential Holmes: Selections from his Letters, Speeches, Judicial Opinions.*

Today's Journal

In what direction are you moving?

_____

_____

_____

_____

_____

_____

_____

_____

What does your future look like?

_____

_____

_____

_____

_____

_____

_____

_____

Action Step – What will you do with these thoughts? And, by when?

_____

_____

_____

Session 48: Fidelity

"Many persons have a wrong idea of what constitutes real happiness. It is not obtained through self-gratification, but through fidelity to a worthy purpose."

Helen Keller

What are some of your ideas about real happiness? Many people would link it to money, as in "do I have enough?" Others might say a satisfying and successful career or a solid marriage. While all of these things might be important at some level, they don't necessarily lead to a meaningful life by themselves because self-gratification is about the ego.

To this writer, having a purpose is a given, but what does "worthy" entail? One could easily substitute words like earnest, commendable or laudable. But these words seem to be more about how others might see your purpose. What's way more important is how it resonates within you.

Do you feel really motivated to pursue this direction? Are you excited to get up each morning with this thought? And lastly, can you say you have "fidelity" to this purpose, which means, are you really committed, faithful, and dependable to this end? Are you really walking your talk?

Helen Adams Keller was an American author, disability rights advocate, political activist and lecturer. Born in West Tuscumbia, Alabama, she lost her sight and hearing after a bout of illness at the age of nineteen months. She is the author of *The Story of My Life* and *The World I Live In & Optimism*.

Today's Journal

Do you find your purpose to be worthy? If not, why?

_____
_____
_____
_____
_____
_____
_____
_____

What does fidelity mean to you?

_____
_____
_____
_____
_____
_____
_____
_____

Action Step – What will you do with these thoughts? And, by when?

_____
_____
_____

Session 49: Mastering

"The master in the art of living makes little distinction between his work and his play, his labor and his leisure, his mind and his body, his education and his recreation, his love and his religion. He hardly knows which is which. He simply pursues his vision of excellence in whatever he does, leaving others to decide whether he is working or playing. To him, he is always doing both."

Zen Buddhist Text

The ability to see life as a whole rather than as separate parts is a gift – but it's not easy. Maybe that's why the Buddhists refer to this person as one who is a "master."

Thinking of situations in an either-or fashion comes from what Richard Rohr calls the dualistic mind. He also calls it "ego-dominant" thinking. The Zen Buddhist master who wrote this phrase is agreeing with Rohr in that a better way is a "both-and" or non-dualistic thinking.

Looking at the entirety recognizes that there is a little of both sides in any argument or position. Pursuing your vision of excellence in this fashion is a wholesome, wise way to live. And it is easier to do this when you are present to life on a moment-by-moment basis. Some people call that "be here now."

And being connected to a Divine Presence, whatever that means to you, probably places you on that spiritual path of purpose.

Zen Buddhism is a Japanese school of **Mahayana Buddhism** emphasizing the value of meditation and intuition. It originated in China during the Tang dynasty, known as the **Chan School**, and later developed into various sub-schools and branches.

Today's Journal

Would you describe yourself as an either/or person or a both/and? And why?

_____

_____

_____

_____

_____

_____

_____

_____

What would being a master of your life look like to you?

_____

_____

_____

_____

_____

_____

_____

_____

Action Step – What will you do with these thoughts? And, by when?

_____

_____

_____

Session 50: Connectedness

*"Man did not weave the web of life - he is merely a strand in it. Whatever
he does to the web, he does to himself. All things are connected like
the blood which unites one family. All things are connected."*

Chief Seattle

Chief Seattle raises a really good point – we're all connected – somehow. Whatever actions you take affect other people, organizations, the environment and many other things – like your health.

Thinking of your actions in this way allows one to be aware that what you do does make a difference. Thinking ahead is not that difficult but does take an awareness of these connections. For example, how fast you drive to work or to the grocery story may not seem like a big deal. But, if you're always in a hurry, you naturally want the other guy to get out of your way. This only increases your blood pressure and may affect how you relate to your fellow workers, your family, or your spouse.

Realizing that we're all connected is likely to be advanced by whatever your spiritual perspective might be. When you recognize that you're not the only one, when you understand that there is a Creator or Divine Presence, that you're not in total control, life just gets better by itself.

Chief Seattle was a Suquamish and Duwamish chief. A leading figure among his people, he pursued a path of accommodation to white settlers, forming a personal relationship with "Doc" Maynard. The city of Seattle, in the state of Washington, was named after him.

Today's Journal

How do you go through life considering that you are connected to something larger than yourself?

_____

_____

_____

_____

_____

_____

_____

_____

Why is this important, or not?

_____

_____

_____

_____

_____

_____

_____

_____

Action Step – What will you do with these thoughts? And, by when?

_____

_____

_____

Session 51: Tradition

*"A reverence for one's own tradition is not incompatible
with respect for the tradition of others."*

Jon Meacham

There are many spiritual and religious traditions out there and most of us have gravitated toward, or become involved with, the one that most resonates with our overall worldview. If one had the time to examine each of these traditions, I think you'd find a fair amount of commonality.

Probably the most common aspect would the recognition of a Supreme Being, called by various names, with "God" being the most common. Prayer is another aspect – a practice – that is also pretty common. Some traditions have rote prayers, others have more spontaneous supplications. Others use silence as a means of praying. And walking in nature and simply communing and listening is yet another approach.

When we scrutinize our particular tradition, we can become even more dedicated to that approach. We know we've thought about it at some length – it feels right. Knowing how dedicated we are makes it easier to appreciate that same kind of commitment that others have for their tradition. Anyone who's serious about their spiritual journey, who has an open mind about the mysterious, knows that others have probably gone through a similar process. That open-mindedness makes it possible to respect the tradition of others.

Jon Meacham is the author of *The Soul of America* and *American Lion: Andrew Jackson in the White House*

Today's Journal

How would you describe your tradition?

_____

_____

_____

_____

_____

_____

_____

_____

_____

What are the common elements you see among the various spiritual traditions?

_____

_____

_____

_____

_____

_____

_____

_____

_____

Action Step – What will you do with these thoughts? And, by when?

_____

_____

_____

Session 52: Willingness

"Genuine spirituality is the willingness to enter into a process of dialogue about meaning, within oneself and with others and to stay with it over a period of time."

Peter Vaill

To many people, purpose is a big word – a big concept really. And in the context of spirituality, purpose is an important concept worth understanding – worth delving into. In my experience, it's a game changer.

For me, purpose didn't enter my vocabulary until I was in my second career job at the **Vail** ski resort in 1974. The company had hired a consultant to walk key executives through "Smile School," a workshop designed to help us relate better to our skiing guests. That was my introduction to **Richard Leider**, the author of several books on the subject of purpose, and today still a friend and colleague.

To be honest, I can't remember to what extent Leider referenced "purpose" in those early workshops, but he definitely grabbed my attention and caused me to get his book, **The Power of Purpose**. I was only twenty-nine at the time and probably had not given the direction of my life much thought – except for finding the right woman.

As I mentioned in a previous session, when I encountered **Werner Erhard** he got my full attention such that I started making the first real plan for my life. At first it was just about work, but when I married the love of my life, Pamela Sue, my thinking expanded. Then we built our own log home on two acres in Colorado's **Lake Creek Valley**, just west of the **Beaver Creek** ski resort. And mentioning Beaver Creek here is interesting because that's what I focused on next – building a resort complex. Before long the idea of building community was in my thinking.

A few years later, the spiritual component of my life began to take shape when I was asked to lead a group in building **Vail Christian High School**. All of a sudden, God was back in my life. I hadn't been to church – except for weddings and funerals – for maybe fifteen years. But when the pastor announced his plan that Sunday morning in 1997, I felt a tap on my shoulder from that Divine Presence.

The spiritual dimension of this story is that I now see I was being led in this direction, but I didn't know it at the time. Someone was opening doors for me – some Source. Now I often pray for the Good Lord to shine a light on the right door – usually among several doors – so that I might be knocking in the right place. Over those years my purpose went from "Building Community" to "Serving Spiritually-Oriented Community." And in my view, it's perfect because that's exactly what I'm doing to this day !

Peter Vaill is the author of *Spirited Leading & Learning*.

Today's Journal

How would you describe your own purpose story?

_____

_____

_____

_____

_____

_____

_____

_____

And what about your spiritual journey?

_____

_____

_____

_____

_____

_____

_____

_____

Action Step – What will you do with these thoughts? And, by when?

_____

_____

_____

Extra Session: Happiness

"Genuinely happy people do not just sit around being content. They make things happen. They pursue new understandings, seek new achievements, and control their thoughts and feelings."

Dan Buettner

Some people think that those who say they are happy aren't really productive. They think those kinds of people are lethargic or not really committed to important work.

I agree with Buettner's argument and see that the key word here is *genuinely*. That word takes one beyond just smiling a lot and appearing to be happy or content. Genuinely happy encompasses being sincere, honest, frank, authentic and honorable about what you're up to.

These kinds of people get stuff done – they make things move. For me, I've always enjoyed creating programs or projects that touch other people in some positive way. And books have always fascinated me because other people's thinking typically triggers something I could be doing to benefit others.

I'm pretty sure I'm genuinely happy !

Dan Buettner is the author of a series of books around the **Blue Zone** concept.

Today's Journal

Does your life bring significant periods of deep happiness?

_____

_____

_____

_____

_____

_____

_____

_____

And more than anything, what makes you happy?

_____

_____

_____

_____

_____

_____

_____

_____

Action Step – What will you do with these thoughts? And, by when?

_____

_____

_____

Wrapping It Up

I hope this experience of journaling has caused a bit of contemplation – an examination of what's important to you. And even though I don't have a Year II journal – yet – I encourage you to remain in the primary question – what is your purpose? And since there are actually many relevant questions, I list some of them here for your convenience.

These are my favorites !

- When you last really examined your life, what did you discover?
- Can you articulate a vision for your next chapter?
- What are you really committed to?
- How does the notion of responsibility fit into your worldview?
- What does "inside first" mean to you?
- How would you describe the condition of your heart?
- What are your most important values?
- How difficult is it for you to be patient?
- How does a spiritual perspective help define your significance?
- What practices bring you closer to your Maker?
- What makes you come alive?
- What do you lose yourself in?
- Have you ever heard from that inner voice?
- What personal attributes do you hold most dear?
- What does it mean to you to lead from the heart?
- How do you react to those who see things differently?
- What activities evoke excellence in you?
- What does the description "divine presence" mean to you?
- In what areas of your life do you feel creative?
- What is your heart calling you to do?
- How would you articulate a vision for your life?
- What practices do you use to look inside?

Postscript: My Latest Collaborative Venture

The Vail Alliance for Purposeful Living, currently in startup mode, inspires purposeful living and helps people manage life's transitions, including the inner work of developing more clarity and self-awareness and the outer work of contributing to communities and the world. The Alliance programs, both online and in-person, support individuals as they navigate life and work transitions and their self-renewal. Through one's own sense of it, purposeful living is sharing, giving back, paying forward, mentoring, and serving others and the community. Our purpose is to inspire purposeful living.

We are all works in progress—some master works, others less realized. All of us are on a journey, in a specific time and place, and with an expiration date. On our journeys, along with our triumphs, we get stuck, lost, discouraged, tired, or bored. Jobs and careers end. Marriages and friendships end. Circumstances change. New interests call. Change is a constant that we must learn to navigate. As young adults, we start with little to guide us in mostly uncharted terrain. As older adults, we know the terrain well, sometimes too well to imagine a new route or different vantage point that would re-spark our creative spirit. Whatever the stage of life, people are often looking for help igniting their creative flame and sharing that heat and light with others.

Meeting the Moment

The gift of this moment (2022) is that everybody in the world has experienced some form of isolation, disconnection, illness (or fear of it), anxiety, and reassessment. The collective experience of the coronavirus pandemic will reshape all of us going forward and may well point our lives in new directions. The launch of an organization that speaks to purposeful living and transitions aligns well with this moment. It's fortunate that Vail has the leadership, commitment, and track record to address these needs and opportunities. The Vail Alliance for Purposeful Living is tailor-made for this moment.

Where do people go for help with purpose and transitions? For many, there's a giant void. Some forage for support from family or friends. Some turn to religion and faith. Others to books. Most go it alone. But isolation can be debilitating. Some transitions are painful and lonely, others exhilarating. People today want to know their lives have meaning and seek help in having courageous conversations about what that means and in making it happen.

The initial program of the Alliance is entitled **RoundTables.**™ These are small groups of 5-6 people discovering meaning, values, vision, and new possibilities and plans, with personal stories, questions, and experiences shared in dialogue. These groups gather over time (e.g., monthly over the course of a year), with mentorship and intergenerational exchanges. Affinity groups based on age, areas of interest, profession, as well as those with diverse, cross-sector representations are mentored through a "wise mentor" program. These gatherings could come in different versions, including fireside chats with outdoor components, workshops, and more.

Unlocking Capital in Vail

"Capital" is often seen as an economic concept: value in the form of money, property, or other assets. Natural capital is the ecological stock of Earth's resources that support life. Human and social capital include value inherent in individuals and their networks. Community capital is the sum of all the above—the collective and interdependent financial, natural, and human and social capital in a place.

Vail creates and contains an astounding amount of capital in all these categories. It's a remarkable community with world-famous winter and summer activities, cultural offerings, and medical facilities with a focus on health and wellbeing. This community is blessed with a remarkable group of successful retirees, CEOs, elected officials, artists, teachers, entrepreneurs, athletes, and professionals of all stripes. Arguably, we leave much of this capital on the shelf in many of our communities, including Vail. The idea of unlocking that value, both for individuals and for the larger community, is compelling.

Join Us

We invite your input and to engage with us.
Join us on this journey of inspiring purposeful living
Http://www.vailalliance.org

About the Author

John Horan-Kates has more than fifty years of leadership experience in business and community organizations. He received an undergraduate degree in business from **Wayne State University** in Detroit in 1967 and subsequently became a Distinguished Naval Graduate of the **U.S. Navy's Officer Candidate School**. Following this training, he served aboard the **USS Jennings County** in Vietnam.

After departing the Navy in 1972, he served as controller for the **Kirkwood Resort** in the California High Sierra. Several years later he came to Vail and served as vice president of marketing for **Vail Associates,** founded the **Vail Valley Foundation**, helped build the **Vilar Center for the Arts,** the **Gerald R. Ford Amphitheater**, and then helped start **Vail Christian High School.** In 1994, John was named Vail Valley Citizen of the Year. In 1997, he helped launch the **Vail Leadership Institute** where he served as president until 2013 and subsequently served as board chair. In 2020, he helped re-deploy of assets of the Institute, re-connect all those participants, and launch the **Vail Alliance for Purposeful Living.**

In 1998, he received a Master Coaching Certificate from the **Hudson Institute of Santa Barbara**. He is the author **The Leader's Journal** and several leadership essays and has published two leadership guidebooks. His other books are **When Called to Serve, A Journey Toward Surrender** and **The Vail Way – The Making of a Community**

He has lived in the Vail Valley with his wife Pam since 1974. They have two children: a daughter, Brooke, who is a real estate broker in Cordillera, Colorado, and a son, Conor, who is a software engineer living in the Vail Valley.

Printed in the United States
by Baker & Taylor Publisher Services